# City Full of Fireworks & Blues

# City Full
# of Fireworks
# & Blues

## Stephen Cramer

SHANTI ARTS PUBLISHING
BRUNSWICK, MAINE

# CITY FULL OF FIREWORKS & BLUES

Published by Shanti Arts Publishing

Designed by Shanti Arts Designs

Shanti Arts LLC
193 Hillside Road
Brunswick, Maine 04011
shantiarts.com

Cover image: Manovector / shutterstock.com

Printed in the United States of America

ISBN: 978-1-962082-11-2 (softcover)

Library of Congress Control Number: 2024932901

For my middle and high school English teachers, especially Mrs. Pawliczek, Ms. Flaum, and Mr. Carulli.

# ‹ ALSO BY STEPHEN CRAMER ›

*Shiva's Drum*

*Tongue & Groove*

*From the Hip*

*A Little Thyme & A Pinch of Rhyme*

*Bone Music*

*A Jar of Moon Air* (translated with Alejandro Merizalde)

*Turn It Up: Music in Poetry from Jazz to Hip-Hop* (edited)

*The Hot Sauce Madness Love Burn Suite*

*The Disintegration Loops*

# ‹ CONTENTS ›

## THREE

# ◄ ACKNOWLEDGMENTS ►

*Allegro Poetry:* "Museums"
*Antigonish:* "Tunnel"
*The Baltimore Review:* "Choice"
*The Brasilia Review:* "The Path"
*Brilliant Corners:* "Soul Station"
*The Brooklyn Review:* "Metal"
*Catamaran Literary Reader:* "Telomeres"
*Chicago Quarterly Review:* "The Hyoid"
*Chronogram:* "Air Guitar"
*Crossways:* "Making Way"
*deLuge:* "Relief"
*Glint:* "Murals"; "Never Be"
*The Lake:* "Sweetheart, You Make Me Feel Like a Spider;
    "Under Stars"
*The Laurel Review:* "Lemons"
*The Loch Raven Review:* "Wishbone"
*The Main Street Rag:* "Temple"
*Offcourse:* "Theories"
*Off the Coast:* "Names"
*One Sentence Poems:* "Distraction"
*Red River Review:* "Because"; "Found in Translation"
*Slant:* "Check One Box"; "Jillicking"
*Sugar House Review:* "My Angels"
*Throats to the Sky:* "Speaking in Tongue"
*Tupelo Quarterly:* "Crepuscule with Joey"; "The Calls
    of Extinct Birds"; "Weather Report"
*Verse-Virtual:* "Whole"

# ‹ RELIEF ›

Every day the atoms
of my body

are a little closer

to being atoms
of something that is

not my body.

Soon enough
they'll learn to sing

from something other

than my throat.
So today, my prayer

goes like this: please,

manifold tribe
that makes me up,

help me,

while you can,
to relieve my mouth

of this song.

‹ **ONE** ›

# ‹ MAKING WAY ›

After so many millions of years
of not being, you'd think

I'd be innately qualified,
a professional in oblivion,

but no: here I am again
practicing how not to be.

I close my eyes, try to feel
my heart not as a heart

but as a stone, my tongue
as a slug in the grass.

I try to breathe as though
each gulp of air

were another root pressing
its way through my chest,

or an errant drop of water
taken in again by the mother

cloud. I used to think life
was a blink, but really

it's the opposite: the flash
of eyes opening in the night,

& the rest... not sleep, not
dream, but dispersal,

permeation or, better, penetration
as the earth spreads its soils,

clenching & pulling
to make way for your bones.

# ‹ THUNDEROUS ›

The sound of a tree
growing in fast forward—

a hundred
years in thirty
seconds—is a brief

recital of rasp
& squeak & groan,

the sound of sheath
after added sheath.
It sounds like ice

breaking up
in the spring. It sounds

like an avalanche. Try
to hear the same
of the entire woods,

then of the continent,
then of the world.

Try to be deafened
by life. I want
to be able to hear

in thirty seconds
all the decades

of my own heart
beating, a rattle
that grows louder

then quickly subsides.
I want to hear

the sprouting
of leaves in the spring,
their crackling

in the fall, all of it
so thunderous

you can't distinguish
the loss
of any one thing.

# ‹ BREATH ›

My breath swirling
the room like
a pollen-drunk bee,

I let the air
slip out
in as slow

a stream as possible,
because that helps
me understand

strength. I've yelled
& slammed my fist
in my palm,

so I already know
what weakness is.
You can spend

all afternoon
trying to figure out
what version of collapse

wants you more
than all the others.
Let us learn

the way cries
inherit our breath,
the way 1,000

facets of song
can inhabit
the mouth.

# ‹ CHOICE ›

Tonight, it looks like the stars
have had a few. Orion

is skinny dipping in puddles,

choreographing sweet dance moves
with a streetlamp. Actually,

everything is clearly intoxicated,

from the scent of rain
laced with pine to the grass

tilting beneath our feet.

Let's face it: as of the most
recent assessment, the day

seems to have had a deficit

of awesome. I mean, even if
the task we've been given

is to make a house

out of a hurricane, to make
walls with the whirlwind,

to board by board create

the floor we walk on,
what choice do we have

but to drive lightless all night

& honk at all the moths?
It's far past time to walk

a shattered sidewalk that hasn't

already memorized my stride,
to speak with an eloquence

that tends to slur

into grunt & groan, time to
all night long hook elbows with awe.

# ‹ MY ANGELS ›

After all that listening
to their pure soprano

voices, it's time to rewild,
time to reset the cerebrum

& musculature back to astonishment.
Tonight, the sky has broken out

all of its tangerine swagger,
& I'm letting it ransack

my bones, letting it become me,
the way rain, on contact,

translates itself into a fraction
of the lake. It's good practice

because one day I'll say
my name so that the syllables

fog up the air, & then
the air will be wiped clean.

I can work with erasure
because the angel on my shoulder

has to tag-team the next.
In this chain-linked series

of wings each is more exhausted
than the last. Let's frame it

like this: I'm a big celestial
employer. They call me

the cosmic treadmill.
Let their perfect little entourage

go baroque & bone weary
because I can't pass up

the universe's continual
double dog dare.

# ‹ TEMPLE ›

You know that second between when you lift

your hand to wave
to a loved one on the street

& when they morph into a stranger, the cheekbones

too high, the gait
all wrong, how about

the moment before the circling crow

becomes a plastic bag
caught in a dervish

of wind, you know that breath just after the spiraling

birdcall & before
the canyon's response,

the moment between Diz's clowning & when Bird

lifts his plastic
horn & cuts him

with a melismatic rush honed to a scold, metronome

crushed by velocity...
I'm trying to learn

to dilate those seconds into temples of sand, learn to

breathe in
that luscious

sliver of the day between when the air first tastes

like thunder, but before
the tree's core is scorched,

all day the smell of smoke ghosting our skin.

# ‹ LEDGER ›

This body is a container
        for a certain number
of breaths, a certain

        number of kisses.
The horizon of your skin
        makes gravity a myth,

releases every trace
        of music stored
in my muscles.

        One day all my thoughts
will narrow to those
        I had in the womb,

the world's vast
        nomenclature stripped
down to basic

        human need.
I know it's probably
        written on air, but

somewhere there's a ledger
        that tells us
how much of our breath

        we've given to dispute,
how much to song.
        Remind me again

how not to be
        a howl on a string.

# ‹ GO AHEAD ›

When traffic lights
conspire against us

we'll transpose them

into a string of red pearls.
Go ahead, universe,

send the biggest,

baddest cyclone you got,
because we'll just

trash talk the horizontal

rain. It doesn't matter
if you send every upturned,

rusty nail through our soles,

because we're a straight up
festival on feet. We choose

to be unadulterated,

USDA unapproved
stamina, sliced & diced,

& our thirst shall not be

doled out in teaspoons.
You & I are pending skeletons.

# ‹ PLAN ›

The choice is this: a grin
          or a sob in every breath,

but I've got a lark
          in the middle of my name,

so that means: *sing*.
          I mean, I don't want to be

the person who plants
          poison ivy, & besides,

blue, today, has decided
          to ride the sky.

Then again, *desire* comes
          from the old French, "await

what the stars will bring,"
          & who the hell wants

to await anything? I mean:
          If I could only behave

I might just hold off
          the silence blooming

around my name.
          I plan on not behaving.

# ‹ CREPUSCULE WITH JOEY ›

The sun's only
half of your DNA

end to end away,
which is part

of what makes
this hyperbolic sunset

the most recently
discovered species

of *what the heck.*
This afternoon

we eavesdropped
on the maple & its three

octaves of color,
so now let's spy on fire

flies, the new dusting
of distant suns,

each off-tempo cricket.
I like the way guesswork

feels in your mouth,
& my fingers

want to trace
every anthem they know

across your spine.
I'm stunned,

a mute man in a city
made of tongues.

# ‹ THE CALLS OF EXTINCT BIRDS ›

I've learned that sometimes
you have to accept that the day

is inside out, a birdcage
built out of birds

imprisoning a ball
of wire, which does not

sing. I've learned
that you can hold

a funeral for every passing
moment, or you can watch

them the way you might
watch a mockingbird

sing in the cold,
the music made visual

in small bursts
of condensation as the heat

of each note hits
the frigid air. I'm trying

to learn that this moment
is not only now

but also everything
that has brought us

to now, the way
the mockingbird's

unreeled repertoire
consists of both

car alarms & the calls
of extinct birds.

It's time to catalogue
all the extinguished

parts inside me,
& all the ways I can

reintroduce them
to breath.

# ‹ WEATHER REPORT ›

Look back through
the hoops & rings

of heartwood, they say,
& you'll find the early

weather that shaped
the tree, the barren skies

that starved, the thunderheads
that fed. Tonight the wind

is made of pine smoke
& tar, & as some kid

shapes a heart
into the new road,

my heartbeat settles
to the trees' memory

of how to let go: gold,
coral, flame, all carving

the dark. How easily
I could be on a first-name

basis with heartache,
my mind corkscrewing back,

but instead the shifting breeze
turns the air into a sweet

bath, & clouds swarm the sky,
not dirty rags but copper

heaps, so sun-shot
that I can't help

but admit it:
my only real job

on this street or any other
is gratitude. I've walked

into a story again, a man
holding his hearing aid

out to his lover's lips
as though he could touch sound.

# ‹ JILLICKING ›

I don't think it's too drastic
to request that normal

behavior come
with a warning label.

Even though, when it comes
down to it, we're all

disappearing with astonishing
proficiency, we're pretty

good at finding reasons
to not do something.

Update: our job is to keep
perennially undisinterested,

to figure out
what makes the intricate

gears that join tooth
& notch to crank the sun

to its zenith, to let
the constellations keep

wheeling. I mean,
anyone can jillick

a small, flat piece
of shale. Let's see

what we can do
with a boulder.

# ‹ WHOLE ›

The wind through this tree
proves that music

can be made from being split
in two then split again.
So today I'm trying

to memorize those
multitudinous rhythms,

trying to let the airy
riffs become my musculature,
calibrate my breath.

Impossible pastime,
but anyway I raise a toast

to the wind, & to all
the miniature obstacles
& mazes we living creatures

make for it: bark & leaves
right down to cicada & flea,

aphid & the noble earth
worm. The wind, divided
& redivided exponentially

by reeds, never stops
trying to recover balance,

rushing into low pressure
like sound filling
your mouth. Gale, zephyr,

squall, gust: my fingers
& legs split them all, as daily

we ourselves are split,
as daily we break & break
because it's the only way

to make of ourselves
music, the only way

to stay whole.

# ‹ MUSEUMS ›

*This field is like a clover*
          *museum*, Isa said, this sage

with five-year-old bones.
          That means that this tree
is a gallery of crows,

so many roosting
          that there's no tree,

only crows in the shape
          of a tree. In a moment,
they all lift at once,

& pivot as one
          toward the lake,

which the wind has made
          into an exhibition
of ripples. Our bodies

are museums of blood
          & curiosity, our heads

rare collections
          of fantasies & fears.

# ‹ QUESTIONS ›

Though I aim
to be a main

contributor
to grief's failure,

I may
or may not

suffer
from etiquette

truancy. I require
little to no training

to make questionable
decisions. I am made up

of inquiry on top
of inquiry. My greatest

hope is that
you'll continue

to want
to hold

all your questions
against mine.

‹ TWO ›

# ‹ BECAUSE ›

Because I'm a skeleton
wearing a few inches

of flesh & some jeans
I'm going to rub my face

on some wild columbine
& learn how to live

on rocky slopes, sing
all the neighbors' stares

into my direction, suck
on this rice like it's a 5

star meal, convert my feelings
into the brass angles

of jazz & then translate them
into words which are less

than the croaks of frogs
& the sadness of white

throated sparrows, make an igloo
of leaves in the fall

the wind be damned,
dance to pop songs about

having sex with money,
scratch my name into a stone

& toss it into the deepest waters
so that it can be rubbed

by an eel, look everyone
in the eye who has been broken

in so many different ways
than me, hydroplane

as often as possible, keep on
not breaking someone's jaw,

put three times
the wrong key in the lock,

be there when the thirsty
river opens its throat.

# ‹ CHECK ONE BOX . . . ›

the form says,
but I can't because

I'm what happens
when the kid mixes

all the paints. Try to
pin me down to a map

& you won't have enough
pins. I'll swallow

your melting pot
& spit out a dozen flags.

I'm the mutt howling
down your door.

My family tree's no tree
but the riot of bramble,

my roots no tap root but
branching, fibrous. People

on the subway ask me
the time in Spanish, the time

in Greek & Italian &
when I answer all my accents

cancel each other out.
Let's face it: if I were xenophobic,

I'd have to mobilize
against myself, turf wars

rumbling in my blood:
knock out a window with a brick,

the note tied to it
with insults in a foreign

tongue I happen to know.
I'm more than a medley:

jumble, mishmash, hodgepodge.
My country's flag

is a patchwork,
more stitching than fabric.

I'm more suture than skin,
& I'm strongest at my seams.

# ‹ WHAT'S HAPPENING? ›

Pardon me, but
you're one of the least

grotesque things
I have ever laid

eyes on, which I feel
is an important fact

to stop & consider.
I mean, in life

you're doled out
a certain number

of raspberries,
kisses, cool sides

of pillows.
Like, can you

even believe everything
that's going on?:

people stopping
at stoplights, people

buying carrots,
etcetera. Insanity!

& that's just the people!
What the heck

are the two-toed sloths
& narwhals up to?

The world is a big place,
& there's hardly

a single speck
where happening isn't.

# ‹ TELOMERES ›

At first they cap the four
ends of our chromosomes

like thimbles. But as they erode
then disappear altogether,

our cells, exposed,
become too run-down,

too frayed to function.
This is called

aging. Sometimes I look
at my body & think

*I have a body,* think
*these are my arms,*

*this is my brain,*
*& I can tense them*

*or let them lie slack.*
Each raindrop is a piece

of light broken
off of the moon.

What part of me is being
ground down,

& what part growing
thin? What a trick

to have been grafted
to flesh for these years.

# ‹ BRIDGE ›

I practice walking
backwards

because that's how
we live: seeing

what's behind us,
blind

to what's to come.
Here we are together,

crossing this bridge
that's anchored

at both ends
only by fog.

What else is there
but to be

& be held
& be beheld?

# ‹ TUNNEL ›

*The air,* Isa says,

*is just like the land*

*except it's full*

*of holes.* On the sidewalk

we breathe the grains

of sky & birdsong

that other bodies

have dispersed.

We shape our hands

into shark fins to part

the air, & what our hands miss

we split with our noses.

We burrow down the street,

taking our time because

burrowing takes time, until

the bus barrels past.

As Isa runs to greet

her mother stepping off,

I try again to see

her world. I glide

into the sleeve

of her path. I smell the fresh

earth of her digging. I tunnel

through the glowing

cavern of her day.

# ‹ THE HYOID ›

The only human
    bone that doesn't touch
        another, you buttress

the tongue, umbrella
    the larynx. 46
        years, & just now

I've learned that you inspire
    the tongue's acrobatics,
        its saliva-slick shift

& glide. Oh winged bone,
    when the day is a tune
        with seven notes

of the scale missing,
    I will think of you.
        You're the way

our bodies teach us
    how loneliness lies
        at the heart

of speech, how we can survive
    suspended between
        bone & belief.

# ‹ CITY FULL OF FIREWORKS & BLUES ›

That's what Isa called
the long sweeps

of orange & purple
that she spent all morning on—

the sky a stipple
& wash of tones, part pulsar,

part jungle gym.
I check back in with her

later, & she's eclipsed
the whole page with black.

It's like the painting
has died. To her,

dying is like stepping
into a closet. You can take

a flashlight with you
& step back out

with a grin.
She doesn't know

the knob comes loose
in your hands.

# ‹ SWEETHEART, YOU MAKE ME FEEL LIKE A SPIDER ›

Sweetheart, you make me
        feel like a spider. Not just
any old spider, but the one I saw

earlier this summer, the one
        who manufactured a coliseum
of a web—do you hear me?:

a colosseum from her own body!—
        between the rear view
mirror & the window

of my car. I didn't have the heart
        to swipe the web away
with a stick, not enough heart

to say, *hey spider, I love*
        *your work, but you've chosen*
*the wrong real estate.*

So I took a mid-summer
        road trip, & with all
the packing & hullabaloo,

I forgot about the spider.
        & there we were 600 miles
& 5 states later, at 75 miles

an hour, & I checked the mirror
        to my left & found not the flaming
red Camaro I expected but

the jeweled parachute of a web
        warped by velocity, the spider
still clenched to its back side.

Sweetheart, I'm trying to get this
        back to you. Well, for the next 100
miles I couldn't help but see myself

not as a simple driver with a home
        somewhere behind me & a vague
destination out in front but as some

eight-legged, more tenacious
        version of myself, &—oh, that's it!—
I remembered that that's how I feel

when you step into the room:
        one minute I'm just sitting there
watching a fly

bang its head against a pane
        the next I'm flying a supersonic
jet without a windshield.

# ‹ UNDER STARS ›

Even when the blues
hexagon by hexagon

fill my chest,

my hive overflowing,
I like the way guesswork

feels in my mouth,

the way my body is high-
jacked by a bassline.

The late night sky,

gone hyperbolic with light,
cradles us & makes me feel

like I've just entered

a sweepstakes for one.
Tomorrow we'll wake up & say

*That was exhausting.*

*Let's never do that again,*
*& I mean soon.*

# ‹ HERE ›

Impossible,
in this continual

tally of undoing,
to pinpoint

that moment when a child
turns adult,

or the moment when
the adult converts

once again into a child,
muscle & memory

obstinately loyal
to their daily reduction.

Everything that's ever
been given to me

will be repossessed,
a harvest in reverse.

Honey, our destinations
are in synch, it's just

that we're all heading
to the same place

at different speeds,
& we probably

won't meet there.
Who knows if this

conversation will be bridge
or wall, but let's make

a date to see
each other here.

# ‹SMOKE›

If the pile of wood
      can be at once

its past as a tree
      & its future as smoke,

then does that mean
      I'm both my first breath

& ash? Questions like this
      are grateful for flesh,

so that they may be
      asked. This voice

is just an extension
      of a burning body.

May all the music
      we make be edged

with the dark
      jewels of soot.

# ‹ HOLLOW ›

Though the world
      is cuneiform,
            & I am the king

of botched transcription,
      at least it goes both ways:
            sometimes it feels

like my wishes
      have been translated
            into Cantonese & then

back into English
      by two people who speak
            neither Cantonese

nor English
      & have then spoken
            those wishes to the deafest

of the gods. It's why
      I've been trying
            to understand

that the world can be
      both mango & knife edge
            not with my brain

but with my heart's
      four hollows,
            the places where my heart

isn't, the places
      that need
            to be filled.

# ‹ FOUND IN TRANSLATION ›

Some days the blues
shadow me like

a badly dubbed

film, lines lagging
just behind the lips.

Don't talk to me

about serenity. One guy
ate an airplane

piece by piece over

two years, but he still
couldn't fly.

Maybe the things

I've believed in most
all this time have been

fossilizing my brain cells.

How much there is
in the world to re-discover:

how the stream pushes

the swamp an inch further
south each season, how

to throw a pebble

at an asteroid. I try again
to understand

your half smile.

Its curvature
is a foreign

tongue I want

to spend the rest
of the night learning.

# ‹ HEARTS ›

They couldn't be more
different—the heart

& the hearts kids draw,
one a complex of volatile

rooms & muscled corridors,
the other two stick figure

ears pressed together
& filled with lipstick. Only one

allows for the vibrations
of the throat, the glorious

mobility of the tongue.
Only one knows the years

are a door, the way the heart
has doors that you can open

a little more every day,
or narrow to a crack.

Since we're made of transit,
a blood cell cruising from heart

to big toe & back in a minute,
we try to let our two stories

spill into each other like a single,
valveless cascade, but more

& more these days we try
to simplify ourselves back

to that childlike vision.
We try to be two ears

pausing, pulsing, listening
to each other's listening.

# ‹ METAL ›

Starved for contact,
sailors traded any last scrap
of metal for whatever intimacy
they could find.

*My chest walks*
*to the rhythm of her stride.*
*Her scent spirals*
*the brainstem, petaling*
*my scalp with shivers.*

They were dizzy with the breeze
full of frangiapani, heliconia,

*the burning striations of the tiger*
*lily in her hair.*

They slept on the ship's floor,
no nails to keep up
their hammocks.

*All my belts have lost their buckles.*
*My glasses are a pair of flat gems.*

Loose floorboards rumbled
where the ship's metal ribs
had been stripped.

*I'd brave that long ocean*
*on a single plank, my teeth*
*pulled out for their fillings*
*& pawned.*

The sailors didn't
look back
at the shoreline shrinking
beneath the horizon.

*My rear view mirror*
*is busted & my brake pedal*
*is covered with thorns.*

# ‹ RE-ENTRY ›

The constant
coloring in

the lines is out
of line, leading

only to cardiac
inadequacy.

Let's re-enter
what we never

should've unentered,
those five-year-old

bodies that knew
the recipe for sky,

bodies that made
an almost endless list

of what the rain
doesn't sound like,

bodies that knew
how to hollow out

hammers & fill
them with birdsong.

‹ **THREE** ›

## ‹ SOUL STATION ›

Tell me what it means
that these days, even more

than tuning into the notes
that furnish the air,

I keep on imagining
the patterns inside the horn,

the dark flowers
of the breath's condensation

as Hank Mobley surrenders
note after note of "Soul Station."

Tell me why I imagine
florets blooming

in that pitch darkness
while outside, now, the fall leaves

should be distraction enough:
their colors part carnival, part

ecstatic advertisement for death.
The music swells as leaves

spin & figure-eight
& pivot on an unseen axis

of wind, so tell me why all I hear
is that exact space inside the horn

just before where the notes
formed, somewhere between

the breath & the bell. Tell me
about how darkness is the perfect

habitat for belief to vine & vine
in spirals no matter how hard

someone has tried to blow
it all out into the light.

# ‹ SPEAKING IN TONGUE ›

My favorite, slick braille,
brined, I read you over

& over, my tongue
memorizing your phrases

multitudinous, amazed
at how much you can say

in such a small
space, amazed at the pink

pendant & two wings
that make very bad

bodyguards but very good
wingmen, or let's say

wingwomen, because
they are strong yet ready

as well they should be
with both of our mouths

open, mine open to speak
the language of moisture

to moisture, yours open
to speak vowel

after vowel, a salty
language that I would

speak all day long,
that I would eat all day long

if one could eat language,
& although one can't

this is the closest
one could come

to doing so,
this is the closest

one could come.

# ‹ NEVER BE ›

I'll never be the seedling
on the telephone

wire that draws sustenance
from nowhere, though daily
I'm shimmied

by the murmur of voices.
I'll never be the sky insinuating

itself between
each wing in the murder
of crows, though I can let it

choreograph my mood.
I'll never be the housefly

buzzing in the key
of F, but I can hum
in harmony. I'll never be

the low-hanging
cloud above the lake,

but I know
that it's really just the way
that something as heavy

as the lake
is learning how to fly.

# ‹ NAMES ›

The long water
rustles inside the sleeve
of itself, & for the mother

merganser alert by
the shore I'm stripped
of titles—father, husband,

son. I'm just the nameless
shadow too close to
her seven ricocheting

hatchlings. Do I know this
stretch of water better
or worse because I know

its name? I imagine
the landscape stripped
of consonant & vowel,

that layer of film
that sullies the world.
Onion grass tries

to go back to its curlicue
of green, Whiteface
Mountain recedes to a glacier-

bitten wedge, the ducklings
retract to feathered
protoplasm. It's useless. *Curlicue,*

*glacier, feather:* the labels
snap back into place,
& the birds fly back

towards their mother,
back toward the safety
of their radiant names.

# ‹ THEORIES ›

I have some theories that revolve around

the swallows' drift
then sudden angled dive,

& others that center around picking up the dry

sticks of worms
two days after a rainstorm.

I have many more about the soft horizon

of your hips. One
of my greatest doctrines

involves the blue weather systems that snake by

at night, although
the starlings crammed

in the eaves, balancing on a banister of light

give it a run
for its money.

Some days nothing makes sense. But then I stumble

into a ditch filled
with the asterisks

of chicory & hubcaps, & the spokes

of some beat up old
bike point out

toward the edges of space, explaining everything.

# ‹ TREMORS ›

Sometimes when I try
to figure out how

you feel I feel
like one of the medieval

monks who painted
an elephant

but had obviously never
seen one, & so concocted

a horse with a long
snout, a boar with a bugle

nose, a nozzled lion.
Elephants send word

to each other
through vibrations

that migrate the subterranean
tracks of the savannah.

How many tremors
do we feel each day?

Let me keep my feet
to the ground. Let me

feel your seismic
changes travel

from my toes
up through my spine.

# ‹ BIOAUDIOLUMINESCENCE ›

I want to play
this song on repeat

until we experience
what we can only call

bioaudioluminescence,
our bodies lit by

the resplendence of air
blown through brass.

Certain notes turn
the skin supple,

because the world
works like this: after

the man hit his head
he could no longer

hear, but he could taste
how you feel. Certain

notes say *how the heck
can you be so down*

*when this day
should be hyperbolic?*

You know, right now
we're as far from death

as we'll ever be.
& if what they say

is true, that you're made
of what you seek,

then I am made up
of the cells of your clavicle.

Because I seek a coalition
with the day, I am

a coalition with the day.
Because I seek

to understand not only
the twenty-seven

bones of my own hand,
I am not only

those bones but also
the hollow bones

of the hummingbird
with the broken wing.

# ‹ IT ›

Try too hard
to grasp it,

& it's like drinking
water with a fork.

Loosen your grip
& it's always

with you, though
it disappears

like the taste
of your own tongue.

# ‹ AIR GUITAR ›

I strum the shower's steamy air,
my fingers pinching a pick

that isn't there.
My job pays dirt, & life's unfair,

so I make chords of my fingers
& shake my hair.

The foggy mirror knows
that I don't care. I purse my lips

with a screw-the-world stare.
My jaw is a vice

& my eyes are a dare.
& my instrument is made of air.

# ‹ MOANIN’ ›

Your hurricane
has tangled my wind

chimes, & I'm not
sorry. It takes about

100 muscles
to speak a single

word, but how many
to push two cheeks full

of air through brass?
The trumpet's message,

delivered over the course
of nine & a half minutes

& multiple
octaves, seems to be

that at some point
the second half of a jump

becomes an orchestrated
fall. Some days

my spirit animal
is rabid, but you can't hear

its moaning, only
my voice. Music implies

that something's been struck.

# ‹ MURALS ›

Let us paint murals across
the buildings—brick, window,

door, & all—murals
of the fields & sky

they obstruct, so that you look
at an edifice but see

everything but edifice.
Let's let asters & cosmos,

bergamot & columbine
reclaim the bricks' space

so that even the bricks
wondered what they

themselves were. How about
murals of high, helixing

grasses on fences so it looks
like you could wade

from a field into yet more
field. Let's make it so

you have to know just
which knot of wood

to stick your key into
in order to open the door

to your house.
Would it not just feel right

to paint SUV's & trucks
with the trunks of trees

so that a highway looks
like a forest in motion?

& if we could paint
over car exhaust & contrails

all the better to turn
those toxic shreds

back into blue.
Let us not hesitate

before V616 Monoerotis,
the closest black hole

to earth, which has no chance
of destroying us before we

get down to that business
ourselves. Let us practice

disappearing our bricks,
our signs, our wheels,

our smoking barrels,
so that we may feel

what it's like just before
our turn has come,

so we may feel our murals
crumble, & imagine

the painted sky
turning back into sky.

# ‹ LEMONS ›

Once a man
got into an accident.

Totaled his car,

which was a lemon.
The truck

that hit him was for sale.

He bought it
on the spot. He stopped

at a kid's roadside

stand & vastly over-tipped
when he picked up

a cool cup

of lemonade, then drove
his new truck home.

Please let there always be

lemonade. Please let the truck
that hits me be for sale.

# ‹ DISTRACTION ›

In the museum
of picture frames, try

not to be distracted
by the paintings within:

incidental lily pond,
subsidiary nudes,

minor skies blurred
by the dizzy churn of stars.

# ‹ WINGS ›

Every atom is only
average or astonishing

depending on
the other atoms

it's currently attached to—
a roadside's rusty bumper

or your hip bone.
The 13.8 billion years

before those atoms
formed our bodies

is a wing. That's why
we stumble around

in circles. We live
& by living try

to excel in the art
of imbalance. We'll only

be able to fly
with the second wing

of billions of years
that we have yet to earn.

# ‹ WISHBONE ›

The waterthrush winds down
      after a long day,

with just enough steam
      to pull dusk into

the sky thread by lilac
      thread. All night long

we unfurl our
      mathematical theories

about the cleavage
      of wishbones, karma

grafted to chance & algorithm . . .
      You say the mouth

is a wound,
      but if it is then two

can heal each other,
      a scar looking at itself

in the mirror. Some lips,
      silvered with fishscale gleam,

supernova a dare into
      your chest. Some say

the body has a stockpile
      of kisses stashed in

its brightest corners,
          a certain number

to dole out to thigh,
          eyelashes, lips.

All I know is
          the kiss unbestowed

shrivels & cracks,
          a dry old leaf kicked

down the street.
          Your eyes

are like a hall
          of mirrors inside

a hall of cracked
          mirrors. That's where

I want to get lost,
          where I stare

into the glass & every
          reflection is yours.

# ‹ THE PATH ›

So many times you're no paved road,

not even a trail
worn smooth

by feet, just a smattering of breadcrumbs

& birdseed scattered
by wind & squirrels.

Some mornings it's hard to say how much

of the sky
is the sky

& how much of it is me looking

at the sky.
Isa says, *I take deep*

*breaths so that the world can have wind.*

My borders
may not always match

the borders of the world, but I try to blur

my edges.
& so you lead

me on, you take me for a ride,

you disappear
altogether, & then

you find my feet again, oh path.

# ‹ NOTES ›

"Crepuscule with Joey" is for Gertrude Higgins. I mean Joanna.

"Choice" is for Matt & Cyndi. Let's get together and hook elbows with awe as often as we can.

"Tunnel" is for Isa, since one of their quotes appears in the piece. Same with "Museums." Same with "The Path." Same with the title poem of the book, which was inspired by the name of one of their preschool paintings. Okay, Isa pretty much wrote this book.

"The Path" is for Mike B. From Westtown to NYC to VT.

"Distraction" is for Alejandro & Christina and our old MoMA stomping grounds.

# ABOUT THE AUTHOR

**Stephen Cramer**'s first book of poems, *Shiva's Drum*, was selected for the National Poetry Series and published by University of Illinois Press. *Bone Music*, his sixth, won the Louise Bogan Award. His ninth, *The Disintegration Loops*, was a finalist for the Vermont Book Award. He is also the editor of *Turn It Up! Music in Poetry from Jazz to Hip-Hop*. Cramer's work has appeared in journals such as *The American Poetry Review*, *African American Review*, *The Yale Review*, and *Harvard Review*. He teaches writing and literature at the University of Vermont and lives with his wife and teenager in Burlington.

# Shanti Arts

## Nature • Art • Spirit

Please visit us online
to browse our entire book catalog,
including poetry collections and fiction,
books on travel, nature, healing, art,
photography, and more.

Also take a look at our highly regarded art
and literary journal, *Still Point Arts Quarterly*,
which may be downloaded for free.

www.shantiarts.com

)